Insecurities Run Your Life

Insecurities Run Your Life

Self-Awareness Today to Shape Your Future!

Cameron Ségard

An Imprint of Segard Publishing

For general and marketing inquiries, please email info@segardpublishing.com.

First Edition

Designed by Cameron Ségard

Photography by Carlos Chavez

Library of Congress Control Number 2020918870

ISBN 978-1-73555388-0-8

Thank you to all who have influenced and taught me what I know today.

Contents

Think For Yourself

There is no one way to live life, and this is just a collection of my experiences and lessons learned that have helped me the most. Use or discard these ideas as you wish, but you will only learn when you listen. Proceed with an open mind

We are not in complete control of our lives which may cause insecurities to distract us from developing a stable future. Identifying how insecurities effect your life is part of the solution, but when combined with purposeful action focused on your values; you can defuse your insecurities and become limitless. Time spent understanding how insecurities control your Personal Life, Career and how you manage your Money will allow you to form the future you dream of. Invest enough time and effort to apply these ideas and you will likely find yourself living a more secure, stable life. I encourage you to write your ideas and notes throughout this book, it is time for you to write your future!

Cameron Ségard

USA, 2020

Introduction

With all of today's distractions, we rarely take time to consider alternate approaches to creating our best lives. To not waste your time, I kept this book short so that you can focus on pursuing your goals. Who am I? Simply, I am just another person trying to become financially secure and confident of who I am. I wrote this book to share what I have learned to be successful and healthy in today's society. Considering that personal values change over time, it is necessary to prepare new tools for the future, so you are ready for your journey. This concept will slowly develop your personality based on what you surround yourself with over years while you define, refine and realize your values. Unlike our clickbait habits of today this process takes years of focused effort to develop. Turn off your notifications, grab your favorite coffee cup, dim the lights, and take a journey considering what it will take to become whoever you want! Nothing stable happens overnight... this book alone will not solve your problems, but what YOU do with the ideas that occur while reading it just may. If you are worried or overwhelmed about the prospect of being completely responsible for everything in your life and how there is no safety net, and by just walking away it all falls apart like a sandcastle in the rain... well, good news, you are not made from sand. In fact your carbon bonds are extremely strong and resilient, you can choose to stand up against your challenges and replace them with better problems; based on what you have learned from your current situation. Much of this looks like and is hard work, there is no cheat code to get ahead in life. Let's get started refining your perspective on life while developing a method so your everyday actions benefit your future. Do not become distracted by the haters and bullies along the way. They are just jealous that you have the guts to do life YOUR way. Keep your actions humble, honest, and most importantly, consistent!

Insecurities Run Your Life

Personal Life

Some days are easier to feel satisfied, while others can feel completely uncoordinated. With all of your past experiences and so much going on day to day, it is nearly impossible to be aware of every aspect that has affected your current attitude. But what if you could guide your future experiences to enable you to become who you want to be? This is possible with routine self-awareness and regular intentional actions, pausing when you feel overwhelmed and taking a breath when you feel empowered. Insecurities from our past keep trying to distract us from becoming more successful today. In balance, this personal feedback can lead to healthy development and growth; but unchecked this could be the cause of anxiety, unhealthy coping habits and unnecessary stress. I challenge you to be conscious of what your expectations are for your current chapter of life. Reflect for a moment: Do you feel satisfied with where you are? Wherever your feelings do settle, your response can be used to shape where you spend your time and mental energy today. Evaluate your response. Am I being too harsh on myself? Are the expectations to which that I am holding myself to causing me unnecessary pain? If I do satisfy those expectations, will I be happier, or will it be to please others? Ultimately you should prioritize what supports your future and values.

In order to maintain this level of life focus, I encourage you to intentionally ignore and remove activities that do not align with your life. Focus on what benefits you and helps others the most as a healthy use of your time.

Some may view this as self-serving, but much of the external feedback we receive in life is not productive or healthy. It is up to YOU to filter out which feedback should be considered or discarded. There are so many avenues for other opinions and approval i.e., verbal conversation, texting, pictures-mostly done through social media. These are nearly all selected to benefit the content generator and rarely show personal struggle. Setting up our minds to always evaluate the difference between our lives and the lives of those we follow, and potentially leading to depression, feelings of inadequacies, and confusion about our current status in life. That is why it is important to carefully pick those whose feedback we choose to follow throughout our life. We all require different types of support during different chapters of our lives, because at each point in time we will be developing a different aspect of who we are. Early on, we are primarily focused on school and receive grades to tell us what we are doing right and wrong, as well as social aspects based on who we hang out with and look to for approval. As time passes, we may choose which topics or fields best fit to pursue our goals regarding college, trade schools, jobs, etc....

Over time YOU repeatedly pick what lessons and feedback you receive, choosing deliberately - not your current environment or insecurities, the beauty here is your freedom to pick the direction you develop by surrounding yourself with the feedback you think is best for YOU. Work to reduce the triggers and distracting sources, and expand connections and input that prepares you for the future YOU desire.

I am not oblivious to the fact that not everyone has the ability or privilege to remove as many distractions from one's personal life as they would like. I cannot properly address this topic adequately within just one book or with just my perspective. But what I do want to encourage is for you to be aware of what is happening around you and try to understand how it is affecting your daily life. To break it down, how does food, sleep, money, exercise, conversations with family and friends, your work environment, time spent on social media, and lastly your time at home affect it? It is not necessary to dig deep into each aspect to see how it impacts you, just simply ask yourself "did that interaction or experience support or distract me ?" Do you feel better after spending time with them or being on that app? Over time, by keeping mental tabs on what adds value and what takes value away from your life, you can begin to remove what does not align with your chosen future as you continue to develop and grow. Remember you won't be able to repeat today, so spend it doing what adds value to what you value.

If nothing else is within your control, you have absolute control over your words and physical actions; so when you are confronted by a negative influence, you can choose to engage and give away energy that could be used to benefit your goals... or step back to defuse the situation and keep your energy for a more beneficial experience. I'm being very literal when I say energy, since how much mental energy are you willing to invest or waste on a supportive or degrading interaction? We only have so much physical and mental energy each day, and that is why you must use it with purpose. Protect yourself from the barrage of distractions and preserve as much energy as you can each day for what you value. Some days will require you to give up much of your energy to others, because they need to be lifted to a point where they can actively regulate their own energy, just as you are. Then hopefully they will return the favor to you some day and make you feel energized too! Taking a moment to care for another human will enable everyone to live a little bit better.

From what I have observed so far in life, we as humans do not talk about mental health enough and allow relentless negative self-talk to rampantly rain down on our own thoughts. We were not meant to be isolated behind phone screens, texting, emojis, snaps, swipes or whatever other trend we think is the best way to connect today. Taking the time to really connect during an in-person conversation is the best way to heal yourself. Now, many mistakes will happen along the way and hard questions will have to be asked. Some topics could be uncomfortable, and others could make you cry as you pursue genuine connections. But this is all natural; expectations that we must always have our s#!& together is just outdated and incorrect. At a time when we can connect the easiest, we feel the most disconnected than ever before. My opinion is, we as humans were not meant to have this much external input so regularly and need a community and ample personal time to support ourselves. If you consider moving to a new city for a fresh start or a new job, realize what you may be leaving behind. You will need to be ready to support yourself in all the ways your community had before and be open to new input from what will become your new community. Change is hard, and it takes time to adapt to your new environment, but if you want that opportunity bad enough, you will endure whatever it takes to achieve it. And by being aware of how your insecurities try to run your life, you can take back some control and direct your future.

1.1 Patience... It Takes Time To Grow

The rise and grind motto is a good analogy for what it takes to really hone your skill set and achieve your goals. It takes years of hard work to secure a stable lifestyle and refine your personal habits. In my experience, it is rarely the few grand actions or decisions that define your life. Instead, it is the impact of your routine decisions on a daily basis-just like a chef's sharpening stone, the fine abrasion of the rock sharpens the edge of their knife. And just like your daily habits, the small actions are the ones that define your future. They enable you to be prepared for the few times you have to perform near your true potential. They allow you to be ready for not only the main topic, but for the left -field questions and conversations that come from it, with the ability to smoothly transition from your area of expertise to the related and supportive information, without a need for reference material. To achieve this level of mastery takes dedication, commitment, and deliberate sacrifice along the way. So, stick to what you love doing and do it well, don't become distracted with parts of life that do not support your values. If necessary, be decisive and cut out influences from whatever source that may be if they prevent you from achieving your goals. Control your time so you can spend it how you see fit to support what you value; be selfish at times so you can do you. But when the pressure does subside and you have time to breathe, don't forget to support others and reach out when they need it. In my experience, you can run fast alone, but you can run farther together. Know how to participate as a leader and a team member. Take time to listen.

1.2 Hydration

Stay hydrated, you will be able to be more productive. It's common knowledge that our bodies are made up of mostly water, so it is obvious that keeping that topped off with water will allow our bodies to work more effectively. Keep a reusable water bottle with you wherever you go, get a sturdy bottle and personalize it or just reuse your favorite brand bottle. Whatever works for you, try to drink at least two to three liters a day, so your body can do a better job at supporting what you want to do. Think about that relationship for a second: you treat your body better so you can do better… and yes, it is that simple. Drink water!

P.S. Coffee and alcohol dehydrate you so make sure to drink some water for every one or two drinks you have to play it safe. Otherwise you'll end up with more severe headaches, which could be avoided.

1.3 Fitness & Regular Diet

You have goals and desires in life that require you to be active and mobile, in fact strong and energized so make time every week to prepare yourself and go work out at an intensity that you are comfortable with for 30 minutes to an hour, 3 days a week. However you go about it, be consistent as it takes years to build and maintain any level of fitness. Think of it this way, investing some time each week into your personal fitness will allow you to do nearly anything you want with your future, and that is amazing.

The phrase ”you are what you eat” is quite true, and it is important to know what your body needs and what it cannot process. Identify which foods your body is sensitive to or does not tolerate; if that is in fact true, then follow up with your primary care provider or a dietitian and check to make sure. What I'm getting at is that we all have unique dietary needs, and doing what everyone else does is likely not right for YOU. The key is consistency, because you can't expect the same performance from yourself if you feed it inconsistently. For example, when I miss a meal or don't have enough to eat the day before, I can feel it the next morning and that changes my attitude and how considerate I am. Supplying yourself with a consistent diet will absolutely provide you with the most stable supply of energy for what you need on a weekly basis. Go find a way to supply your body with what it needs, however variegated or bland it may be.

Eating fresh food is critical for your development, and many studies show how this plays a big factor in your overall success in life. While not the final factor by any means, the better fuel you give yourself, the better you will perform and feel. This does not mean that you should only buy organic food, it means FRESH food. Minimize how much processed food you eat and limit or eliminate food groups that do not agree with you. Consider the following: Dairy, Gluten or Eggs, which may not agree with your body, and which you are likely already aware of. It is up to you to find out what is the right amount of which foods for your diet.

I will say if you are a regular at any restaurant, however fun that may be, it often is too much food for a routine meal (given typical American portions) and does not have your best interest at heart, quite literally. It's a business and they are out to make a profit. Now, it could be a social event, and those are critical to happiness and social engagement, just be conscious of what you order if you do go out to eat on a regular basis. Stay healthy friends! Make sure to explore new foods by trying new restaurants when you do go out, make it an event to reward your hard work.

1.4 Modern Media Influence

Considering how our American society has rapidly evolved recently, it has caused more confusion of how to progress through life, because the traditional paths are no longer accepted as the norm - particularly the lifestyle changes between our grandparents' generation, for example, and our generation. Their lives were more structured and typical of their time compared to modern life today, which can be more personalized but appears to be less structured. I think the major change was the massive increase in cultural awareness due to media becoming so prevalent, and its exposure of world problems and epidemics available to the masses today. Many of these problems always existed but were not as readily publicized to the world as they are today.

This distracts all of us from our local community problems, in addition to the challenges we all individually face in our lives. So be aware of how much media content and which sources you choose to follow, as they have a strong impact on your attitude and consume your valuable time. Both of which are among the key drivers to make secure rational decisions day to day. Be active in selecting which content you choose to consume while staying abreast of world events; without giving excessive time to news stories that do not directly change your daily life. In my experience this approach has helped me eliminate a lot of distractions that would have kept me from focusing on what I value on a day-to-day basis.

1.5 Distracting Yourself From Progress

How do you cope with stress? Do you structure your time to achieve your goals, or do you fall back on old habits of pleasure, infatuation, binge watching, eating, drinking, traveling, etc... to make yourself feel better fast? No one can operate without emotion and only follow a strict plan, but it can be helpful to recognize when you are using those coping mechanisms. This allows you to ask yourself why am I doing "X" to feel better, which may highlight another area to spend time thinking about. We all should treat ourselves now and then to what we enjoy, but this is specifically geared to prompt you to think about how you cope when you are stressed. The difficulty is that life throws multiple problems at us all the time, and our emotions and thoughts can be confusing and volatile. It requires active thought today to process why you want to do "X" when there are so many factors that could be causing that impulse.

1.6 Quick Quotes

- Don't undo on the weekends what you have worked so hard for during the week.
- Prepare for the worst and you are the most likely to be successful.
- Smart work can beat hard work if you are consistent and have a plan.
- Seize the moment but do not dominate the conversation.
- Be willing to fail today so you can be successful tomorrow.

1.7 Independence And Relationships

A definition of Independence is : One's ability to be content while being challenged with the various things that life sends your way, without a dependency on mutual support or guidance from another.

Notice, I did not say "happy" to define being independent, as our society has told us too frequently that we must be happy to achieve our dreams. Instead, I like to think of it as finding a comfortable, stable, routine mental state, not too low (sad, demotivated) and not too high (happy, zealous). While you are content, you will be able to make rational decisions and evaluate complex problems that come your way, to make positive impacts on your life and the life of others.

Recall that you are in the process of shaping YOUR future every day with each of your actions. Under a distracted state of mind, you may be constantly anxious or worried about what you don't have control over. Finding peace with what you cannot control and investing your time in what you value will be most constructive.

Before you can focus on anyone else, you need to have found a stable lifestyle and routine. Identify where you need to improve yourself and own up to it; blaming others for your past will not solve your problems today. However justified you may have been, and however good it makes you feel to blame... forgive and release the pain. Harboring it will only grow resentment and consume you emotionally. Write your emotions out, try to cope, use whatever constructive methods are available to help you get to the position to improve yourself (like what this entire book is talking about). Once you are comfortable with where you are, push yourself to a new environment and test what you have just built. Be proud of your success and growth, no one can take that from you. You will be mentally stronger, more focused, healthier by taking time to care of yourself. This process will continue to cycle every year of your life to varying degrees of difficulty and success, constantly give yourself attention and build yourself up to a state where you feel prepared to support others.

Before you should invest time to become a part of someone's life, you need to have found a content mental state for yourself. Do not go looking for another person to satisfy what you have not addressed adequately. I am not suggesting any state of perfection, but address what has hurt you, so that you don't hurt them. It is not another person's job to pick up your life or make you happy, you must own it and maintain that yourself. While they can help support you as you chase your life goals, they are who they are. If they have bad habits or traits that you do not like today, or they make you feel bad, those are not going to disappear overnight or possibly ever! Pause and think about that for a second... So be real with yourself when it comes to dating and considering who is a good fit for you. Do you have to constantly explain the degrading actions of someone you are seeing to your friends? Do you think that if you give enough love to them, they will become happy? Some may argue that relationships take work and one has to commit to others to help themselves, to get better with known outstanding problems. These "red flags" become more clear as you get older. Most people you meet will not be the right fit and/or the timing will not be right. But one thing is always true, and that is YOUR choice to place your personal value into the hands or opinion of others. Don't let others who make you feel insecure distract you from what is most important - and that is YOU! The challenge is that these triggers may come from toxic forms that you have never processed previously, forcing you to say no to someone that made you feel so good before. It may hurt and distract you in ways you have never felt before. All these lessons throughout your life will prepare you for your future and make you more self-aware of the impact that others have on your self-confidence and metal health. Prioritize time for yourself, so you can have your necessary personal time and are not constantly distracted by comments or activities throughout any week or day. You alone will have to work to maintain your metal and physical health. Listen to yourself for the times when you need an outlet and be willing to listen when others need one too. If you support others, they may support you too! Try to be mindful of who is benefiting more from spending time with you. Are they always listening to your problems, dreams and woes, which benefit you, or are they benefiting from you too? Is it a balanced relationship? How much thought should you put into making sure they feel supported too? Is this additional anxiety or drama in your life worth it to make sure your partner is happy? If it's not close to a completely natural fit, then it is going to cost you a portion of your established content routine to incorporate them into your life. It is up to you to decide how much change is appropriate to include them in your future, as the process repeats and evolves over time.

Be aware if either YOU or YOUR potential partner is still carrying unaddressed baggage from past experiences and are seeking a fix via another person's support. Regardless if that comes from a physical or the emotional connection, know what you are looking for! Are you ready to handle the emotional needs of another person in addition to yours? Do you want to find something that is casual and fun or slow and serious? How open to new experiences are you? The empowering aspect of dating is that you can choose what you want, to satisfy your current needs and desires. Spend some time by yourself to discover your habits and trends. While you are reflecting, see if your interactions only benefit you or others too? Does your current routine reinforce beneficial personal development OR negative habits that cause you to repeat past mistakes and relive negative memories from your past? Be aware of what healthy habits look like for those whom you want to date and see where you two can connect. Make yourself desirable so you have options to consider and are not just chasing one person. It is also relevant to spend time reviewing what you wear, so you are confident and attract who you like. Then you will be assured of yourself when you are around potential partners and be willing to take a chance. Don't over think it, if it feels right go with it; at this point the worst they say is no. Introduce yourself, find a connection and see what happens. Faking anything to impress someone is a self-defeating approach, as you will likely become unsatisfied and depressed with that approach. Be yourself to a fault, and the right ones will laugh with you and the wrong ones will laugh at you (Pay attention to how they respond!!). Being you all the time is the best filter for people in your life to help you weed out the distractions. If they don't like it they won't stay, and that will save you time to focus on what you value, so you can become the best version of yourself. Your independence will enable you to meet whom you should and live the life that supports what you value. Craft yourself and your environment into who you want.

Dream big and work hard, you deserve it.

1.8 Expectations

Honest discussion of what you expect will drive what you take away from your experiences more than the actual experience itself. For example: walking into a dive bar expecting a fancy restaurant will not satisfy what you were looking for, while walking into the same place expecting to see your friends, to catch up and laugh over a dinner could happen at either restaurant and make for a good time. My point is, focus on what the environment will provide and don't dig yourself into a hole by expecting more than that location or person is likely to provide. This begins to address personal expectations, which is a good way to avoid dissatisfaction and frustration when It comes to social relationships. On this same topic, the majority of issues that come up in any group activity are differing expectations are particularly due to lack of open communication. Gasp! This could lead to conflict or strife. No, we can't have that!! Everything must go smoothly so our neighbors or family think everything is perfect; we "NEED" that perfect story. Well, bad news Tinkerbell, this isn't a fairy tale, and nobody can read minds, so we must tell each other what we want, because otherwise it probably won't happen. Hopefully, you are with others that are open to your input and do not drag you to things you don't want to go to all the time, while being cognizant of reasonable compromise so everyone has the experiences they want. Your personal happiness can't become the paramount priority of the whole group, that is selfish. Obviously, there is a multitude of ways for this to spiral out of control, but without continuous open dialogue it most certainly will. Grab some popcorn and enjoy the show! Considering what you convey will influence future decisions and actions, it is important that you communicate honestly. Take time to develop a complete thought and not half-baked idea before you throw it out there, as it's going to cause a reaction. Many times, a poorly processed idea is worse than taking the time to say what you really want. Clear communication is always best.

Remember to date yourself before forcing others into your life so you can say you are "dating". Prioritize your mental health, know your self-worth, and act like it. The right people will make time for you; others will give you time to become who you were meant to be.

1.8.1 Relationships

The majority of them are not going to end the way you may expect them to. Realize it will take time to meet someone else that has a compatible personality to yours. Timing is a really big factor and nothing worth having is easy, so expecting that it will all unfold like your favorite rom-com is adorable, but not realistic. Sorry to rain on your fantasy parade, but dating will take just as much work as your diet, career, home life and then some, I assure you. Just try to find someone that laughs with you and not at you when you do something goofy. They should lift you up and not intentionally ask for more than you are willing to provide when you are feeling down. What this means is that most people you meet will not be the right match for you, and (deep breaths) may require each other to change some to make work the relationship work. Gah serious commitment and risk... no, I cannot handle that... stop it, you probably can. Stop being afraid of what you have not experienced and really look at what you want. What are YOU comfortable with right now? Are you willing to make a change for that person? How well do they fit into your current life? Most people project their fears and worries during any conversation, so it is easy to unintentionally pick up those as your own also. If it is overwhelming, drop that baggage, you actually don't have time for that. Life is too short to spend it trying to solve everyone's problems, it just takes time to meet the right one that you are compatible with. Be honest with yourself and reflect on your experiences to get a better idea why each relationship did not work. Then keep trying, admit what you know you are not good at and be honest when a mistake is made. In time you will find someone that understands and is willing to stand by your side. And during the honeymoon phase of the relationship, take your time, attempt to moderate the physical connection because that can distract from the real interpersonal connection of a stable relationship. Also use the correct amount of protection based on what you and your partner are comfortable with, after establishing consent. There is only one beginning to each relationship, so make it a good one. Listen, share, explore, support, travel when you can and go eat some good food together as often as possible. Trying new food together is a great way to sample foods from different parts of the world without the complications of traveling there. Most importantly don't overwhelm them, allow them to be free. Enjoy what they share with you and stop trying to force something to happen. Be aware of these factors while not losing focus on your own goals and routines that support you. My understanding of a healthy relationship is two people that are independently content, who share their time to support each other. When you do find someone that meets your standards, invest as much time as you should, to see if they are a good fit. Take some risks and laugh as often as possible, while keeping your lustful desire in check. This way you do not disappoint yourself if things do not go as you imagine or fantasize about... I don't know what you are in to 😉

1.8.2 Family

You don't get to pick who raised you and the environment they provided was not perfect, there were oversights and social aspects that you were not exposed to which make you unprepared for some if not many aspects of life. I do know that they provided the best environment for you that they knew how to at that time, and it is now up to you to accept where you are and take responsibility for your future. Holding resentment for their decisions will not help you get ahead in life and I do not want to marginalize those experiences. Many are traumatic and take years if not a lifetime to process with or without the support of a therapist. But I challenge you to understand how those negative experiences have impacted you so you can address them appropriately as soon as possible. Go take the adverse childhood experiences (ACE) questionnaire on the CDC website for more detailed information and do as much research as possible, making you knowledgeable about how your past impacts your life today. This will begin to help you understand your reactions to some of what life throws at you, because you will have a better idea of why and where some of your traits come from. It will assist while you defuse and deflect what alerts you, minimizing how often you repeat the negative experiences to which you were exposed while growing up. It may be that you are programmed to fulfill the negative outcomes which you think stigmatize you. To stop this, you may have to live a very intentional life that avoids or excludes environments which cause you to repeat these self-fulfilling characteristics from your childhood. I am no expert on this topic, but I want you to know about the ACE questionnaire so you can live your best life. If you resent me for bringing up your childhood, I encourage you to look into the reason and answer that for yourself. This was included to increase awareness that these traumatic aspects of a childhood can cause lifelong impacts, whether either you or your partner have these experiences. The more knowledgeable you are about one another's background, the more supportive you can be. Give to the world that which you wish to receive.

Family Tradition, Faith, Culture, and an individual's Sex all play factors into what expectations a family will expect from any individual. What is different for every person is their choice, conscious or not, to conform to what they are exposed to while growing up. As anyone does, they may want different things than what their family is willing or able to provide. It becomes your responsibility to go out and find what fulfills your differing interests; some may be supported while others may not be. What is important to you is the balance of what you choose to eliminate and what you choose to keep as part of your life. These decisions, however mundane or redefining, may require you to leave home and your established support system while you achieve what is best for you. Are these new experiences valuable enough for you to make that change or take that chance - whether it be for a job, college, a lifestyle change, or a partner? It's not my place to tell you how to rank your priorities, but I will encourage you to be very thoughtful before making any big changes. Do you have the money to follow through with it? Will you make enough money after said experience to pay off any debt that is accumulated during it? Are you really prepared to the best of your ability to handle what you will now be responsible for? Do you have a support system in this new environment to supplement or complement what your family can provide? How fulfilled will you be after or during this experience or change? Does a future with said change provide a stable livelihood that validates your interests and passions? Answering these questions individually is not necessary, but allowing the thoughts they prompt to influence your decision process may be helpful to you. Take your time and process this.

Ultimately, I want to help you address and mitigate any insecurities that your family and childhood may have imposed on you during your life. Many of these insecurities are formed and fueled by social expectations baked into what your family expects, so take the time to process what you want vs. what is expected from you. This may help you identify what insecurities exist to which you have not given enough thought, allowing you to address them as necessary while you achieve the contented life of your making. Be genuine and be willing to do anything necessary to make the life YOU value!

1.8.3 Lifestyle

One of the most difficult decisions is what you expect from life, based on what you have overcome to get where you are today. In short, we expect that the harder we work to achieve the social status we have, the more entitled we may become to the next level, because intuitively that is the next step for us. Unfortunately, that is not the case, as you only have access to what you can afford with what cash you have today. This becomes a challenge when you begin to participate in a lifestyle that you can't sustain or support consistently, be it through expensive hobbies, trips, events, notoriety, ect. You naturally like the additional status and attention that you receive, and you want more of it. This can seem like an addiction where you lose track of what it is costing you to participate, and causing you to spiral as you continue to try and satisfy your desire for status and comfort. Left unregulated long enough, this may cost you thousands in debts and dearly in friendships that are solely based on materialism and events vs. actual connection and mutual support. If you choose to create a more sustainable environment where you do not become dependent on what you cannot afford, then you will not become so dissatisfied. Lifestyle can be used as a social status indicator because that is what you can pay for today. Is social status all about money? No, it is not, because your personality, demeanor, location, friends, and connections in your town make up your social status. But many of the activities that make up what you do on a weekly basis require money, so the better you manage your money, the higher the social status you can maintain. You may have to wait before participating in the next desired social status until you have saved enough to do so responsibly. Money enables you to choose what you want to do, and gives you more freedom with your time.

If this frustrates you, remember there are

plenty of rewarding activities in life that do not require much money, and then ask yourself if you are tryingto live above your means. Think about what or who has told you to expect more from life based on what you have achieved so far? Were these promises realistic, based on your level of perceived success? I hope this inequity of these mistaken expectations fuel you to work harder at shaping your future, and keeping your aspirations in check along the way. The better you manage your lifestyle expectations the more consistent a life you can achieve, thus enabling you to control where you spend your money, and enjoy your resulting social status. I don't think it is easy or immediately validating in the short term to live within your means, but it is the most sustainable and rewarding in the long run. The challenge is, we all want to be present and engaged in the moment, so we feel satisfied and supported today which, in turn, can complicate finding a social environment that supports one's responsibility and celebrates it. The trick is to find what balance is right for you, and that aligns with your future. How much are you saving for the future vs. how much do you spend today? Lifestyle expectations represent a critical factor in life, and by aligning your actions with the future you value, over time they will enable you to have the lifestyle you want. When you invest your time wisely, your money also supports your interests instead of distracting yourself from them. Do you spend money to distract you from where you are today as a coping mechanism, or in a constructive fashion that enables the future you want? Spend some time setting down your own lifestyle expectations, so you do invest yourself, your time and your money where it supports a future you value.

1.8.4 Society

It is rare that society will reciprocate the effort you invest in your life, when your actions do not align with what your environment expects from you. In this case, you would be going against the grain and standing out from the established norm. My question for you is, do you want to be genuine and rebellious to some degree, or conform and satisfy the expectations your environment hasestablished? I predict that you want to be a little bit of a rebel and make a statement with your life. The question is, have you built a foundation to support who you want to be? To do this, you must remove the interactions that detract and demotivate you from your path of progress and replace them with supportive influences. Finding the balance between what society expects you to do and what validates who you are is a constant challenge. Isolating yourself to follow your path is not recommended long term, as you will still have to interact with the rest of society, and there needs to be a level of decorum and normalcy in place to be successful. In my experience, conforming to appropriate levels of respect and courtesy when interacting with anyone is the best way ensure a positive experience in nearly any social setting. Take some time to refine your social skills and manners, so you can play in any social setting. During our lives, we will all interact in casual and formal environments, and your ability to observe and adapt to them will be pivotal to your reputation and establishing connections. Treat others the way you want to be treated. Don't be surprised if you are excluded from an environment or scene because you were not able to, or chose not to follow the established norms. I'm not saying it's fair, but this is the way society functions; you as an individual are responsible solely for how you engage with your surroundings. It is not the duty of your immediate environment to adapt to your norms. You must be flexible and responsible for how you treat others. In short, you must be mature and deal with others fairly and accept the treatment and comments from those who don't agree with you. It will not be easy, but the future you want is worth the effort through the validation received; along with the adversity experienced along the way... will, fuel your fire.

1.9 Alcohol

Like many things in life, moderation is key;

weather you choose to drink or not is up to you. Just ask yourself whether the environment and mental state you are in, are supportive or generally positive when you drink? Do those around you listen and uplift who you are or try to distract you from your goals to have a good time? Responsible consumption can help develop strong lifelong connections, but abuse can drive you away from what you value and damage relationships. Having experience trying various drinks can be a fun way to connect to others and talk about what you have tried which can be a good conversation topic that many can relate too. Most importantly if you find yourself the only one having a drink or the only one not drinking, just be considerate and patient, it can loosen people and the atmosphere up for a fun time. Just be aware of the environment you are in and if the norm to is to drink or not, this sets the president for who is following the social norm. Many opinions circulate on this topic, so just be considerate to others if they decide to have a drink or not. In many parts of the world or in your country and likely within your town, there are differing expectations about alcohol. When this is not clearly stated, it may not be obvious to most what is the established expectation. Take a moment and communicate the norm within your social group when you are around new people. This will always result in a better outcome than judging someone for their actions when they didn't know they were being evaluated. Having honest and upfront conversations will help ease any differences you may run into.

1.10 Addiction

If you are trying to break an addiction, take action to address your insecurities that are causing you to look for that fix. This will put you in a position to help you overcome your habit developed to compensate for previously uncontrolled factors of your life. You may be using it to try and get ahead, gain social status or just feel better about yourself in the short term. I challenge you to structure your life to achieve said levels of satisfaction more constructively. Anything that happens fast is likely not a stable way to build a foundation. That is all I want to help you build, a solid repeatable approach to life that does not require you to depend on any substances to sustain it. Except for coffee as it is the elixir of life and how I was able to write this book.

1.11 The Grind To Your Future

On your journey to become the best version of yourself ,you may find that you end up working alone quite often to achieve what is most important to you. You may ask where all of your friends are during these times, and simply they are doing their best to achieve their goals just as you are. Use the ideas that you have had while reading this book to enhance your mental toolbox and push yourself to new levels of focus and motivation that you have likely not sustained before. The habits you develop are just a byproduct of you choosing what future you want and defining the expectations you choose to satisfy. Conforming to the work ethic expectations of your peers may not enable you to get ahead. If you want anything bad enough, then you will have to find a way and make time for it. Now take your new thoughts and be more insightful into your life and actions. Be self-aware and active in how you want to shape your future. Work hard, be kind, humble, and consistent!

You’ve got this!

Career

2.1 Leverage Your Knowledge With Education

Your education enables you the freedom to pickwhatroleyou have in a business. Many hold resentments against those who have more opportunities to choose what they do and ultimately, how much they make. Here is one way to give yourself more choices when it comes to your profession. Do not get education confused with just college or school or even knowledge. Your education can come from many sources ranging from family, mentors, work experience, life experience, and hobbies who are sharing their knowledge with you. The challenge comes when employers uses formal education as a candidate selection filter over your obtained knowledge. The approach I recommend is to apply your informal education / knowledge to obtain your formal education to secure an interview. Then you will be able to present your well-rounded skill set confidently because it was built from the bottom up and refined to match your chosen profession. It is not a fair system because others may have had more access to informal and formal education growing up ,giving them more privilege and freedom. You could choose to harbor that resentment and underling insecurity of inequity, letting those feelings infiltrate your personality and generally distracting you from your current situation... OR, you could choose to focus on what opportunities you do have and leverage your current abilities to continue developing yourself. The short of it is you must start somewhere and decide to better yourself at whatever age and perceived socially economic status. My best advice when it comes to learning from others is having endless gratitude to appreciate every piece of feedback/lesson you receive throughout your life while you accumulate more knowledge. Accept that you may just don't know "x" and consider the possibilities if you to a different approach next time with an open mind. If incorporating that piece of feedback improves your life or the lives of others, you should start doing that; it's that simple. So many get distracted on their past, lamenting, blaming, self-limiting, and generally just wasting their time compared to leaving it in the past and moving on. Choose to let it go and focus on what you can improve on today! NOT tomorrow or next week... RIGHT NOW, what can you do that will give you a more stable home life and future? Life can be overwhelming ,and it's hard to cut out the noise and secure time to develop yourself. Stop doing things that prevent you from improving your life and get your time back... You may be thinking, "But that's not what my friends are doing?? I want to have fun with them"... are they bettering themselves for the future or just masking their problems with events and parties? You will have to get over not blending in or participating in things going on today and do what is best for YOU. Protect your time with fervor and entitlement because it is your time to choose what you do. You may not have been aware of how much of your time you were putting your life on pause, but you have control over the play button. It is time to hit play on pursuing your dreams.

Chase a dream that gives you undying passion and energy.

2.2 What You Do Really Matters

Your ability to provide what your employer needs enables you to cultivate and grow what you want at home. Aligning your passion with what you spend the majority of your week doing is pivotal to finding a sustainable profession.

2.3 Well Marinated Used Car

You must get back and forth to work reliably so save yourself some money and drive your current or used car to work for as long as you can. Why... you will not spend time at work thinking about your new car or where you parked it. Your daily should be a car you can easily forget about and use as a tool to get back and forth to work. In some work environments, it is beneficial to uphold an appearance, but this is up to you to decide and how you want to engage in your work culture. This would also be an expense to take into account when considering accepting the job. Does the job pay enough for you to fit the image they are looking for while you are meeting your savings and standard of living goals? It is all a balance, but I would always recommend driving a well-maintained used car. On the topic of cars, the usual deciding factor of when it is time to replace a vehicle is when it costs more per month in maintenance vs. how much it would cost to buy a new to you/used version of the same model car you currently have. So, if you are putting more than $250 or $450 a month in a car to keep it running. That could be enough to cover payments on a less than five-year-old replacement vehicle with some money down that does not require as much maintenance as your previous vehicle. Every car depreciates, particularly daily drivers, so don't get carried away spoiling yourself IF such a purchase takes away from another part of your financial plan.

Remember, this is part of your growth phase and not the rest of your life. Your current car might be a little boring today; get over it. What's not boring is NO CAR PAYMENT and knowing you're not upside-down in a car loan paying some ridiculous interest rate. You won't have to drive a cheap car forever; use it as a tool until you can afford to buy the car that turns you on when you turn it on... That is when you know you have the right car! Just to be sure though, if you cannot walk away without looking back at it; then you got the right one. The trick is to just wait until you can pay CASH for that car, it is a reward to yourself for establishing such a stable foundation. You can then share it as often as you like at cars-n-coffee, cruise-ins, or just dive it and keep it nice.

2.3.1 First Career Opportunity

It is likely not going to be a perfect fit, and you are going to learn more about yourself going through this experience. Business is far from perfect; the majority of the plans do not go as expected, so don't get overly attached if it all falls apart. Successful projects take hard work by all parties and good leadership from the beginning. My recommendation is, unless your role is fundamental to the success of the project do not change your life or vacation plans to give it more of your time. If you feel compelled to spend your own money to buy equipment that the business should have bought; do not, it will never be reciprocated. Work through the correct channels to buy it with approved funding sources. Some personal businesses and entrepreneurs will risk everything to make a project successful, but we are talking about established corporations/businesses with existing supply chain procurement systems. If they do not have their purchasing process running smoothly and getting supplies on time, that is an internal issue that needs to be fixed, and it won't be with your money. In fact, it will be enabled by you not working through the correct channel to improve the existing process.

2.4 Work Culture Awareness

What is the work-life balance expectation where you work?

Do they encourage selfless commitment to the job at hand or recognize the needs that families have and allow you to support what you value? Adapting to what they are looking for while you are at work will work to your advantage as long as that investment does not detract from your energy and willingness to live your life outside of work. Ultimately what this has told me is how well a job or company fits with what I need at that time. Over time, this factor will encourage you to stay at a given job or go looking for another. Like any relationship, it must be sustainable, and your efforts must be properly compensated/reciprocated. In a job context, your pay will be a metric of how much you are willing to work and sacrifice to complete your tasks. If you are passionate and well paid, you may be willing to sacrifice your personal life, vs. only doing what they pay for and not putting in any extra effort. Stating any hard rules here is just not applicable to everyone, I hope you stay aware of how work makes you feel and find an environment that fits you.

2.5 Reporting Progress

Don't say you have made more progress than you have knowingly made on any given task; this may give management the incorrect status for them to make decisions with. Being honest upfront may require more work in the short term but will reflect much better on your reputation than misleading the team, for them to only find out later that you are behind. The real problem that this causes is miscommunication with your leadership; complicating funding, schedules, and etc... planning are all made with the wrong information, and objectives are not met. Because incorrect information was shared vertically due to external pressure, and now everyone is worse off for the initial benefit of saying a project/task was doing better than the truth. While I scaled up the impact for this example, it still holds true for any status report. Honesty in the workplace is pivotal to the success of any team and business.

2.6 Maintaining An Open Mind

Solutions come from the most unexpected places, do not close the door before you have considered the idea. Particularly in that moment, write it down to think about it more later. When you are not in the same mindset, you may realize that such an off the wall idea is ok.

2.7 Let Your Work Do The Talking

This is not a complicated concept; just don't be arrogant and pushy about what you do. You have been studying and practicing for this for years, and you know your stuff. You don't have to be in someone's face to get the points across, just the facts. If they choose to not agree, explain the risk of not implementing the solution or accounting for a known delay. Then move along and let them process the options, if it is critical, then hold the line and make sure it happens. Just don't damage a relationship over it, connections make and break a workplace. The results of the team's actions will speak volumes for your recommendations. Overtime, your input will become valued and integral to the success of each program. Patience is key to pulling off the humble hustle.

What energizes you and keeps you motivated during the longest of projects, particularly when nothing is going your way? Many go through evolutions of what calls to them; ideally you can find a calling early in life and chase it early in life and ride that wave into your full-time profession. While deciding can be intimidating, it should be comforting.

2.8 How Do You Present Your Ideas?

Think about presenting your ideas in the mindset of the consumer of your product/service. Is this in terms that they will easily understand and connect with to make decisions with? Will they want to continue to come back for assistance on these topics or tasks? You're always selling your solution to whoever you work with, work on how you pitch your ideas. Excessive "spin" will work against you as it will seem you are trying too hard, but no spin or explanation of why to use your idea could make you seem unconfident.

2.8.1 Work Smart Not Hard

Educate yourself to a level greater than you have to routinely use so you can work in your comfort zone and are not stressed as much by what work throws your way. Although this takes more time to achieve this level of expertise, compared to just learning enough to do the job, it enables you to grow within your role faster and at a more comfortable pace. Naturally, this leads to the idea of lifelong learning, and if you can get ahead in the specialty, you can then use that advantage for a long time as you continue to develop your skills along the way. How does one go about this? Make reaching that level of Mastery or 10,000 hours of experience your priority, to the point it dominates your time and life at times. Be willing to sacrifice for it and be undeniably passionate about it. This is the ether that will keep you motivated and focused when times get hard, and the progress seems to stop. Your dedication in the beginning, will make your future success seem natural. As you work on your 10,000 hours, be willing to take other jobs to support your career focus. Much of the time it is when we are not focused on a single problem or idea that we have the biggest breakthroughs as we consider different perspectives. Don't stop yourself from working odd jobs to support yourself as you prepare yourself for what you truly want to do. This may demotivate you because you are not doing what you want today, as that is was society told us what success looks like, drop that expectation. If you are working towards something that makes you happy and supports your lifelong goals, then that is what you should be doing today. I want to help you defuse any insecurities about your job, career, or whichever chapter you are currently in; on your path to becoming a master of your field. Trying to satisfy what others expect you to do is not a rewarding way to evaluate your success. Stay focused on what you want to achieve and the path to get there while placing as much time as you can into your future career as possible. In short, get ahead and stay there with the skills required. Then you are not excessively stressed or overworked and can deliver your product/services reliably. If you want to achieve your goals enough you will be willing to do anything!

2.9 What Do You Contribute?

There are many personality types in the workforce, and you can choose if you provide solutions or place roadblocks to progress. Being aware of the emotional state of your coworkers is a priceless talent to have; it is quite likely they are upset about something outside of work that is making them behave the way they are. Possibly they are strung out and overworked near the verge of burn out, and they are just reflecting that stress on you or your team. It is now your task to help defuse that person's stress by being accommodating and providing constructive feedback on the task at hand. Do not focus on trying to fix their external problems directly; that is not your role but instead, work with them to enable their current task is successful and does not cause additional tension to their life. "But it's not my responsibility to be accommodating of others existing problems!" "They should be able to handle their stress and be professional all the time." Sure, in a perfect world no one needs any support and we all have a sustainable balanced life. The reality is our emotions and thoughts don't get compartmentalized when we walk into work. It all mixes together in a big mess called life. If you can help make work that much better for them it's possible that they can get a handle on their situation and become centered again. This is your opportunity to be a leader, the same approach can be extended to your personal life as well. Try to provide a supportive environment for whatever is stressing your friends and family. A little bit of support and compassion can go a long way in keeping a team focused and motivated. If the team is healthy and stable, they'll have the best odds for success.

2.10 Know When To Push It

Growth opportunities come up all the time to get ahead in our lives; it is your responsibility to understand when they present themselves and capitalize on them when they do. It is difficult because your insecurities of being labeled a workaholic or being a social misfit may make you second guess if you should work those long days. If you know that you can make effective progress and you feel focused, do it and do not look back. Write your plan of attack (mentally or literally) and achieve as much as you can before resting to do it again the next day. Hopefully, this wave of focus and progress stimulates itself as you get closer and closer to your final goal. Allowing your success to perpetuate itself as you pursue your goals. Remember this is your life; leave your mark, and inspire others to do the same.

2.11 Stop The Bulls#!&

When someone comes to you distressed in a panic to solve a problem, how do you react by nature? Do your actions perpetuate or stop the uncontrolled environment that has now flowed around you? This isn't about being hypersensitive to some social media trend, this is about stopping the bulls#!& from people who are unprepared. The best way to turn the lack of planning around is to break the problem down. Start with the following questions... What is the problem? How much time is left to solve it? What is the current understanding of the issue? It is critical to separate yourself from the source of the panic, while you are working to orient to the problem and solve it. Ensure that you communicated your estimated time of completion, this establishes a level of accountability to reassure them. If they are able to contribute to the solution, they should stay involved; otherwise it may be better if they take a break and come back later. Give yourself the power to control who is involved in the solution process to expedite it. Take the time you need to do it right the first time to avoid mistakes, which is the primary reason to create an organized plan to solve the now clearly defined problem.

2.12 Communicate When You Need Help

While working in a team it is critical to communicate realistic delivery dates and understand the workload on the overall team. Without accurate time estimates leadership cannot provide the resources needed to support the current program schedule. When you feel overwhelmed do not feel that you are incapable of doing everything asked of you but realize that it may not be realistic at times. Those are the moments when you need to offload tasks and be cautious about taking on additional responsibility. Say no when you need to. This does not mean you are weak, incapable, or lazy; this means you are human and there is only 24 hrs in a day. No matter how skilled you are there is only so much you can confidently deliver every day, and they hired you for your judgment and quality work. As a professional it is your responsibility to determine what can be done adequately and what needs to be done accurately. The 80/20 rule is good to reference, the last 20 percent of any task takes 80 percent of the time and vice versa. What will not do the team any good is if you do not ask for help and end up quitting or switching departments. The team will lose all your tribal knowledge that is not documented and that is what makes you valuable in the short term. Manage your insecurities when it comes to feeling overwhelmed and meter your response, so you do not force yourself to quit. You will be surprised how easily this can happen. Communicate your status to your leader, then focus on what you can do best in the time available. What you do not complete in a single day just proves you are human. The challenging aspect of this advice is that everyone has different opinions of what overwhelmed/overworked is to them, so reference your work environments definition before calling for help. Finally trust your gut on when things are not in balance, instinct helped us as a human race get to where we are today for reason. Instinct and intuition can set you apart from your team, trust your experiences.

2.13 Choose A Challenging Environment

If your environment does not constantly encourage you to adapt to new situations, then your skill set will stagnate. Constantly sharpen your skills by working on new problems just outside of your current comfort zone. You will surprise yourself with how much you will continue to learn as you adapt to your new normal. This goes along with the mindset of a lifelong learning; your prior education taught your how to learn and solve new problems quickly. Recall all the days your studied new material and regurgitated it on a test the next day, every quiz, every test and every final... Were trained to do it every day we are in school, so don't be surprised that is how business works as well. CEO's are constantly expanding the limits of what the current company can produce, which means their current workforce is likely solving new problems every day. How can we expect each development project to go as expected, we can't frankly... But that is where our background and ability to continuously learn come in, your 10,000 hours of practice reinforces your instincts and solutions roll out just in time. This process is stressful but will develop you into a better person and teammate, nothing good happens without a little bit of pain along the way. you were educated to know how to learn and solve new problems.

2.14 Know How Hard You Can Work

Just like a tachometer on a car shows how

hard your engine is working, or the thermometer on a grill shows how hot it is. It's important to know how hard you can work and for how long without breaking, then you have a reference to how hard you are working on any given day. I think it is healthy do try it at least once a year, to get an idea of how hard you can routinely work. But what do you reference hours worked, cups of coffee, hours of sleep?? I challenge you to use your mental health as barometer to evaluate how hard you can work, for how long. I know it's not easy to measure but I think your mental health is what will truly limit how long and how well you can work. Essentially, I'm asking you to test your personal grit; or one's ability to consistently overcome obstacles to pursue a larger goal or objective. Lay out a clear plan with a truly excessive number of tasks to work on sequentially and test how many days in a row you can work towards your set goal, personal or professional. It will not be easy or comfortable, but it will be rewarding and that is what will fuel you to keep going. Your objective is to find out how many hours each day you can work repeatedly and still be effective. Working all night or so long one day that you can't come into work the next is ineffective. You'll accomplish your goals with a steady pace and consistent attitude, persistence will solve your problems.

Plan, Prepare, Commit and Pursue your goals.

2.15 Speak Your Environments Language

In many different parts of the country and levels any business there are common phrases and sentence structure that will make anyone blend in. It is your challenge to decode this unspoken norm and adapt to it, in fact leverage your awareness of how it changes to improve how effective your input is in any environment. It will take time to become aware of the subtle differences between various backgrounds, education level, geographic accents, phrases, colloquial and more. But as you do, it will begin to open more doors and opportunities for networking that were not available before. Primarily because you will reflect the norms of your environment and that gives you a platform to communicate change in a more appealing presentation. It is much easier to make a positive impact or make a convincing sale if you are viewed as one of the team and not an outsider, however harsh that may be to accept that will be your best approach to instilling change. This also gives you a chance to learn more about the group and build an appreciation for the language of your current environment. If you are driven to instill positive change this is your best approach, solve from within.

2.16 Work Life Balance

Only give as much to your job each week as you are willing to take away from the rest of your life.

Think about that for a minute...

The first factor I have seen take team members down is not being aware of their own mental health. Every business or company will always ask for more regardless of how much you can give. For a few months you may be able to sustain ambitious or stretch goals but at some point, we will all crack and require a brake. Once an employee's moral begins to degrade and they feel overwhelmed and do not make time to maintain their mental health. After this point they may still be effective to some degree but their longevity in the team will begin to decrease as this continues. Everyone has different needs so their self-care methods will be personalized. Some will require time at the gym, yoga, hiking, road trips, fancy nights out, cooking, material items, reading, drinking and etc.... Granted not every option is sustainable or fits your financial goals let alone long term personal health. Even when you do care for yourself, we may be taking away from another factor of life. It is common to become depressed or anxious while working hard, but it is important to understand why during these times and find a sustainable way to cope with such discomforts. Not mentioned here is the time required to support a relationship, a family and raise children. Everything we want takes time or money to support.

Make your time at home so valuable and supportive that you want to make it a priority and not give all your energy to your job regularly.

I am not saying give as little time to your career as possible because that is was enables the rest of your life. Your goal is to find the balance that works for you, while you prioritize maintaining your mental health and not just making as much money as possible. Nobody likes working with a resentful or bitter coworker, so choose to not become that person. Your goals and priorities should energize you so you can find the energy to put in the extra hours in whichever facet of life you value the most. The hours invested at home and work will likely cycle like the seasons do, so take it all in stride and keep your priorities in check. Work hard when it feels right and take time off when you need to. Some employers will align with these values better than others, but that alignment will guide you to find the right job for you. With the advent of common telecommuting, if you need a minute for a nap, water the plants, you name it; take the additional flexibility and add some value to your typical workday. The blending of work and life will become difficult to categorize some days, roll with it; and adapt.

For those just leaving college, the next aspect

to be aware of is understanding what, work-life balance is. The balance aspect is likely foreign to you since in college you lived and worked with your friends in class and on the weekends. No real hard separation between studying and partying, tasks can be done at any hour of the day much of the time with the same people. It is a good time while your there, but it can be difficult to translate to a typical work week. Where your work hours are usually set, and you do not typically party with who you work with regularly. You want to make a good impression and solidify your place at work, putting in long hours and trying to be perfect. Your carrier goals end up overtaking your personal priorities and you end up with an extinct social life and the balance aspect looks more like, living to work. To avoid this wonderful spiraling experience as many do; take a note from your seasoned coworkers and how many hours they work and when they take time off. Find a good mentor/example to follow and learn from what they do and how management reacts when they take time off. We want to learn from others and avoid what causes tension. If you cannot find a mentor, become the mentor you didn't have to your team; encourage positive self-talk and the idea of success. During the most dire of times you will become the light that the team looks to for inspiration and motivation, lead quiet and steady and you facilitate success. Have foresight to prevent problems before they metastasize, and your value to the team will become priceless. Allow that energy to enable you to stay humble and focus on the solution that will support the next deadline. We want to learn from others and avoid things that cause tension. Every stable job is a marathon, and you want to be in it for the long haul and not sprint out ahead and collapse because you cannot hold the pace. We only have so much energy each day, each week; use it wisely. In other words, you will want to work smart and not hard regularly, to meet the expectations of your work environment.

Money

It is time to discuss money, because it is typically a taboo topic outside of some friends, family or possibly a financial advisor. Money makes the modern world spin, and keeps the electricity on, but society really does not openly discuss how to manage it. In my opinion that is because many of us associate how we use money with not only external political views that can polarize our country but our actual freedom of choice. That is because money is commonly used as a barometer of success and we evaluate each other with it, intentionally or subconsciously. Your ability to properly manage money for long term goals is more important than your perceived level of success today. That is likely the same reason why some unintentionally mismanage money in the hopes of finding a quick path to the "top" taking a chance on a "good deal" that may net a large profit. I am not saying some more risky and opportunistic options don't work, but I will say they are not as reliable as proper management and allocation of available income during each stage of life. Everyone is not delt the same hand to play with at the beginning of life and it ends up being your responsibility to try and even the odds. Depending on your initial socioeconomic status and where you want to be, you may have to work extremely hard to realize your goal. Expecting the world to provide your success and security is a self-defeating expectation. Therefore, it is important to be aware of your insecurities and prevent them from running your life, there is too much at stake to let external influences determine your spending habits. You have dreams and aspirations which motive you to develop yourself; to make those dreams a reality you will need financial stability and consistent personal habits. Ideally this will all result in the future that you have defined and put the time in to earn. What tool can you use to decide where you choose to spend your money, how would one monitor if they are spending their income appropriately? I like to think of it as financial health or one's ability to consistently align their personal values and goals with what income they have available to spend. There are many ways to approach this topic with varying levels of risk, whether it consciously decided or not. At the end of the day, if you want to save for the future and ensure stability you cannot spend more than you have made each day. While this goes directly in the face of popular consumer culture which always encourages replacement of the old and dependency on the new. You may ask yourself; how will I keep up with the proverbial" Jones's" and all their new cars, phone, clothes, or whatever material item you want to subject yourself to comparison. Well this is the time to become aware and realize that it is pointless to compare your situation to anyone else to determine your own success. Why? Well, it is not that social status or perception does not matter but simply that your financial health is more important to your future than any short-term status or experience. This is the point where insecurities play a potentially fundamental role to all your actions and decisions to date. We make decisions to "fix" what society told us does not align with what norms we have accepted or have been normalized too. You end up spending your hard-earned money to maintain that norm, and you become uneasy when your lifestyle is too far from what you are told it should be during each chapter of life. Really process this for a minute, why did you make your last major purchase? Who did it benefit the most? Did that purchase improve, maintain, or negatively impact your financial health? Be active and purposeful in your daily choices, they all add up and shape your future.

None of this directly has to do with how much money you make; it all has to do with where you choose to cultivate and set your expectations. Whether they originate from your family, friends, school etc.... Forget what level of success you think you have obtained and take a real look at your financial health and what lifestyle that can truly support. We are going to compare what you make vs what you spend and save to see if your expectations are helping you get to where you want to be or if you are working against yourself. Right, now go add up and write in the margins or on a separate note pad what you make, spend, and save on an average month, maybe you don't know. How much of what you pay each month is in interest (excluding mortgage payments)? Let's define interest quickly. Interest is money you pay for money you don't have to pay back. Hold up a second... that makes absolutely no sense, why would anyone want to pay more for something, when they already do not have enough money today? There must have been such an influential outside factor that it became such a priority to spend money you don't have today. Now if it is due to an unexpected repair or emergency those unexpected costs sometimes have to be financed to make life work, but let's lay out a plan for you to avoid paying interest by building an emergency fund as your next priority. What caused this financed purchase, the desire for a new TV, car, clothes maybe your old one broke and you did not know what to do. It is likely that you thought you were more successful than you actually are (sorry, tough love) and could afford to spoil yourself with items you did not have cash for today. Spoiler if you do not have the cash to buy it outright today you need to reevaluate your priorities. Considering you likely just contradicted yourself with your actions because you either applied for a loan or used a credit card to make said purchase. Because you thought you would just pay it off in the future with today's success, well you likely haven't and now you're moving away from your goal of financial stability because you were not patient enough wait until you had enough cash on hand to buy it outright. External influences and marketing made you want to spend more than you currently have, to achieve a desired status. Oooh I own a new car look at me, make sure you follow me, I look like I have money. It's all a vale of deception and you are the one getting taken advantage of in the process by your own choices. You are working against yourself by repeatedly financing anything. It feels good now, but it is doing nothing for you in the long run, nearly every purchase depreciates and now you are spending extra on something you can't afford to have today. Literally you spent money you don't have to compensate for an insecurity which DOES NOT HELP YOU address the insecurities you have. That is like going to the doctor with a broken arm and coming home with a pet cat to make you feel better. YOUR ARM IS STILL BROKEN, you did not fix the problem. It is time to adult and take on whatever it is, sit down and think why did I finance/want to finance a purchase? Was it to distract yourself form a negative environment at home, work, your personal fitness, possibly depression, or to suppress your anxiety? What was so impatient about making that purchase/decision to compensate for said insecurity? If you purchased said item will you have the means to maintain and care for it correctly? Maybe all these points are triggering your insecurities and you just want to stop reading... well if you do, I guarantee you will move further away from your intended personal or financial goals. It is time to face the music and understand the tornado that life has spun for you. What this boils down to is that you must own your insecurities in every facet of life, no one else is going to address them for you. However much you pay or distract yourself with short term experiences of any flavor.

How do we sift through all of these distractions and find a path to financial stability? Well first let's talk about who you want to become... age is not a factor here we always dream and aspire throughout life, we are all free to dream! Write it down anywhere on this page, who do YOU want to become? Where do they (your future self) live, what are their hobbies, do they inspire others? Next, do your actions today consistently align with who that person is? Do you feel more or less comfortable thinking about life when you get closer to becoming that person? You are looking for a reinforcing environment that does not include self-harming habits. Sleep on this and list out your goals, this will help you set your financial path to success. What we are looking for is the difference between who you are now and what you want to be, you decided that you are comfortable becoming that person today... so start preparing to be that person TODAY. With your current understanding of what you want to develop you will lay out a plan to achieve your goals.

Here is how it works...

Let your insecurities tell you what you need to spend time working on. Not by immediately reacting, but in a productive long-term approach, observe what makes you feel uncomfortable day to day; and implement correction action to make you more comfortable. Think of it as a gauge of how content you are with your current environment. This helps you set your true compass, so you find your proverbial "happy place" or at least the path in which you feel that your future aligns most with what you want to become currently. Because while our current environment impacts us in the short term, we are working today so we can improve tomorrow by trading our current problems in for better problems tomorrow. If these recommendations are taken into practice that's what you will find, better problems tomorrow compared to what you have today. The interim comprises of eminence amounts of work, long hours, excruciating self-control, and patience, so much patience. I get it, you want it all today (I do too) but this world moves at a surprisingly slow pace, so for you to get what you want tomorrow usually means trading more than what you currently have to get it, via paying interest, sleep deprivation, physical effort, time with your family and friends. The path that has worked best for me and which is sustainable is one that is consistent, steadfast, and empowers you. Extreme effort today works against you just as much as it benefits you in the short term. The goal is to find a weekly and daily routine that is repeatable to ensure you can make as much progress tomorrow as you did today. Why? So you can plan on your daily progress towards your future better problems. At its core you have likely always wanted a consistent validating life the provides you with empowering experiences.

If you don't address your insecurities, they will build up into a burden so great that it is possible you will be completely consumed by compensating for your insecurities. It's not my business to tell you what those may be, but I do want to give you some suggestions of how you can establish and maintain an environment where you can address what makes you feel your worst. Not necessarily physical pain or the most mentally painful but the ongoing nagging feelings that make you feel depressed and inadequate. That is the sandpaper of life that literally and proverbially wears you down. It is like going to the gym and always skipping leg day, we all see it and know what you should do but you just don't do anything about it. Because you think you are too weak to improve. In fact, you have the most room to improve because of how undeveloped that part of your body is, emotional health or financial health is the same way. Maybe shaming skinny legs is too superficial but let's be honest we all appreciate someone who is in shape. Make time to take care of your mind and emotions too! Mental health and physical fitness parallel each other via regular exercises. Eat healthy food regularly and know your metabolism, this will also be reflected in your grocery bill. Once you find a routine diet that works stick to it with some variation here and there but that is another way to help regulate your routine expenses. We all have to eat so why not eat the right foods so we can get fit and be healthier and happier in the long run. Being healthy enables you to live a better life, invest time into understanding what makes you feel dissatisfied, so you have more time to live! Living above your means today makes your life worse than it would be if you were just patient enough to wait until you were out of debt and had the cash to do what you originally wanted to do.

Let's discuss why this is the case and how you can avoid the oppressing resentment that spending more than you have generates in your life. If you're in debt and you want what you don't have the cash for, we all want what we don't have at some level; this is an ongoing struggle we all face. In various ways we all recognize the difference between what we have and what we don't. The key factor in how it impacts your life and if you are willing to wait to participate at that social status or if you are willing to accumulate debt to obtain that level of material or external perception today. Staying to the point, by taking on more debt for short term gains will more than likely not lead to the future you genuinely want.

To achieve that goal without spending money you do not have will likely take much longer than you want to wait. It is a balance between what you have expendable cash for and what you want to do with it. It takes serious self-control and patience to reach that level of personal finance focus. Just like personal fitness requires a weekly consistency, as do your spending habits. Binging one day a week on any muscle group will not make up for the years that you did not maintain your personal fitness. In all cases it takes repeatable constant maintenance to improve your fitness and financial ability. What is your financial ability? Banks and lenders look at your credit score to determine your payment history and how leveraged (how much you owe vs how much you make) you are in proportion to your current income. Your goal should be to have a good payment history and pay your credit cards off every month. I can imagine that you may be blaming either me or your past for imposing these constraints on your life and you just want to live the life you want TODAY. Well that is not how you get ahead, the interest you pay on the desires you have today with cash you don't have will keep you in your insecure situation for longer than it would be if you just waited for what you want. Yeah your past has likely reinforced all the wrong habits up until now and it is up to you right NOW to decide if you prefer where you are or if you want to change it. Now after years of paying interest and not paying down your debts you resent paying taxes and the bills at the end of the month, you resent those who seem to not have the burdens you do. Frankly, you are just less happy because you were impatient to buy what you could barely afford yesterday. Your situation is not unique and is very comparable to those who waited until they had the cash to buy what they wanted. The difference is they were less satisfied up until they had what they wanted, and you were less satisfied after you got what you thought you wanted. Society and media played you into getting what they said you should want at the phase of life you are in so you could satisfy a social expectation society set for you... Now if that does not make you frustrated as you reflect on your previous purchases you likely are in a good financial position. Established financial expectations have changed significantly over time and the advice from the past will likely limit what you want to do more than you are comfortable with. To get ahead you must find out what is best for you, how much money can you save before you are unable to sustain an acceptable level of happiness determined by your life experiences. It is quite a simple approach that requires you to be responsible, do not spend money you do not have, pay off the debts you may have accumulated and minimize your expenses to minimize the time you are paying off your debts. This way you can maximize the portion of your life where you have financial stability. The only debt that is acceptable in my opinion is a home mortgage which should only be taken if you are comfortable properly maintaining the property which is usually one to two percent of the home value every year in addition to the mortgage payment, utilities, insurance and property taxes. In addition to having a minimum of ten percent down payment, and to avoid private mortgage insurance (PMI) if at all possible;

by placing more than twenty percent down. It's not that you can't get a mortgage with less than ten percent down, it's that you will be paying so much interest vs principal that it's not very efficient. More than likely if you can't put more than ten percent down you are not ready to own that home in my opinion. Think about it like a bet, you vs the bank; and you got into the mortgage with the least down and owe basically everything to the bank. What odds would you put on yourself for paying it all off on time? You likely don't want that much stress and insecurity, so wait another year and save up some more money for your down payment. Or possibly take out a smaller mortgage on a less expensive home to start with. Your mortgage should not be a stressful part of life, if done correctly.

These personal goals take a long time to

achieve, and that is normal. Do not become uncomfortable because you don't have what some of your peers have, because they lived a different story and experiences than you have. You lived a different life than they did, so don't measure your life against theirs. It takes dedication to save for a down payment on the house you want! There may be interim options to buy houses that are starter homes but there is usually a compromise that is taken to settle for it. Be proud of the progress you have made implementing these sustainable habits, as you grow your financial ability. Once you have come to terms with this sustainable financial approach you will see how much more value it adds to your life vs living above your current means today. While this will invariably trigger various insecurities, they are manageable and controllable compared to the ongoing interest payments of literally paying to compensate for your various insecurities that you have not begun to address. And that is why living above your means today will make your life worse tomorrow.

Deep breath, you can do this! One day at a time! Keep up the hustle and believe in yourself.

3.1 By The Numbers

Approaching your financial management habits by the numbers will help you regulate what you have so you can support your future. Don't be intimidated about collecting your various financial figures. They are likely already provided to you in bills and bank statements. Many of your expenses repeat and can be easily tracked to forecast how much you will be paying in the future. This allows you to develop a budget to gauge how much of your income will be allocated to your known repeating expenses. The key to developing a budget is accepting where you need to cut back spending and increase investments/saving so you can achieve your financial goals that you have set. The next challenge is really following the budget, and staying close to your chosen spending limits. Minimizing how insecurities impact your life will drastically improve how comfortable you will be while following your budget. Then you won't be distracted by short term needs, impulse purchases and emergency expenses that could be avoided by structuring your life to support stable mental and physical health. This approach pays back in long term stability and security vs short term validation and infatuation; accepting this financial growth pace will reinforce your life structure and create a solid foundation to strengthen your self-care and financial habits. This is just one way you can help yourself and family by living on what you make to provide the best life and environment possible. Defeating financial instability is in my opinion the key to stable mental and physical health enabling you to stay focused and prevent existing insecurities from excessively influencing your habits and future.

The simple objective of tracking your finances is to generate feedback to yourself on your current financial health. To help you answer simple questions, did I spend more than I made last month? Am I saving enough for my upcoming expense in the coming months? This is just a simple indicator to help you save and prepare for your future. Let's break down each category and fill in the linked spreadsheet you can download (see page 121 for a QR code to scan) to get an indicator of your current financial status. Then we will discuss which categories can be adjusted to achieve your savings goals established by the future you desire. Overtime good financial habits and occasional adjustments to the spreadsheet line items, will help you refine your spending habits and ensure you realize your goals.

3.2 Building A Stable Budget

Before we discuss your finances further, I would like to explain what I mean by using the word stable. Usually we think of stable and steady, consistent, without variation, or a foundation which makes up the basis for things to grow off of. My chosen method to develop a stable budget is to include as many reasonable factors as possible within it. Each factor represents a different portion of your life and or what you are responsible for. This allows you to model it by how much money it costs or makes you to include it within your life. One can use the lowest expected income with the highest level of expenses to predict how much you may be able to save and support each facet of your life. A very safe option. Alternatively, one may predict the max one anticipates making in a year and the minimum expenses they intend to have. A risky option. That decision is ultimately up to you to make and rationalize how conservative or optimistic you decide to be about building your budget. I will recommend that you use the most realistic and up to date values possible to give yourself the best feedback about your current and future financial health.

If you include each budget factor of your lifestyle accurately and follow the values which keep it balanced your finances and resulting lifestyle will be stable. Like previously discussed, when unchecked insecurities can make decisions that your finances will likely not be in a state to handle such unexpected events. Which will potentially incur secondary insecurities and spiral until you take corrective action and realign yourself with a stable budget and lifestyle. Forget what expectations you had about where you thought you would be at this point in your life is an important part of implementing this financial approach. Read that again. The money you can save today will not have an opinion of how you use it. Release what your expectations are and take a good look of where you are by the numbers. Review if you are saving enough for retirement, paying on loan interest, car maintenance, student loans, and particularly lifestyle. Why lifestyle? In my opinion this sets the rest of your expectations and expenses or more directly your perception of how much you "should be spending" to maintain a social status. In turn, this scales how much you spend in all of your budget factors. By maintaining your image at the country club, favorite bar, to meet your partner's expectations, friend group, family, or at work; you may be letting outside factors control what you do. That is why it is important to be honest and accurate when building and maintaining your budget, so you know where all your money goes to work solving today's problems. In time all your work today will help you find better problems tomorrow.

3.3 Budget Spreadsheet

Scan the QR code below in Figure 1 to download a spreadsheet I have developed over several years of personal use. Save your copy somewhere secure and keep it up to date.

Figure 1: Personal Budget QR Code

Now for some very stale but particularly important topics. Probably time for a coffee. This advice is meant to be safe for anyone, so feel free to improvise if you don't agree. It is your money after all...

3.4 Budget Line Items

Gross Income : How much you regularly make on a yearly basis before taxes. If your income is not regular due to several jobs or changing hours at work, look at your past three months, calculate the average and multiply by four to calculate an estimated yearly income. This may not capture a high-income month each year, but it will give you a good indicator of what you can plan for upcoming months and following years. Those readers that do have a typical salary-based job excluding any overtime or bonus from this entry into the spreadsheet. The idea is to plan with what funds you can depend on making going into the future. This will allow you to establish what your income "foundation" is so that you can distribute it to benefit your future, and minimize insecurity fueled spending.

- Last Year's Gross Income :

Federal Taxes Bracket : There are various ways to approach paying federal taxes and I will only recommend the safest option. Which is to claim "0" on your W-2 which effectively gives the federal government all of their tax money up front, so you don't have to pay more when April 15th comes around each year. With the addition of not having to worry about how you are going to pay your federal taxes. You may also receive a federal tax return because you gave the government more money than is necessary to pay for your portion of federal taxes. Depending on how much you deduct from your gross income with pretax investments, federal tax deductions or donations you may be able to "shelter" your income from taxes. This allows you to potentially decrease which tax bracket you are taxed at for that portion of your income. The tax system is tiered where for each segment of your income you are taxed at a different rate, simply as you accumulate income over a given tax year you will pay a higher % in taxes as your income accumulates. These % change over any given year and need to be checked on an annual basis. If you find yourself on the edge of a tax bracket you may find that you can save a significant portion of your income if you can decrease which final tax bracket you qualify for. You can do this through tax deductions or donations that can be written off. It's much simpler to not give this much thought while you are in the saving and growth phase, and just go about your life where you can earn more money else where. It's likely that you aren't making enough to spend an excessive amount of time tracking taxable deductions. If you are that is great, find out where you can deduct from your taxes legally. Some choose to not have anything deducted from their income and save to pay their taxes each fiscal year. If you are willing to take on the additional work to manage your expected taxes due each year, then you may be able to grow some additional income if invested correctly. Otherwise you may end up owing more than you have and that is not a desirable outcome. Choose what you are comfortable with.

- Last Year's Federal Taxes Due:

Effective Tax Rate = Taxes Due / Gross Income

- Last Year's Effective Tax Rate :

State Tax Bracket : Same story as federal but is typically at a lower tax rate depending on location, claim nothing on your W-4 and expect little to nothing to come back from your state tax return.

- Last Year's State Taxes Due :

Effective Tax Rate = Taxes Due / Gross Income

- Effective Taxes Rate :

FICA Taxes : or Federal Insurance Contribution Act essentially, the Social Security (~6.2 %) and Medicare (~1.5%) funds so all U.S. citizens have guaranteed income after the age of 67 to help support an individual's retirement expenses since they no longer work full time. FICA taxes have been around 7.6 % in the past few years as of 2020, check what is withheld on your paychecks to be sure.

Health Insurance : How much you pay monthly for your personal or family health insurance premium + deductible for regular doctor's appointments. This helps you capture and predict what your future expenses will be.

- Monthly Health Care Cost :

Auto & Home Insurance : How much you pay monthly for your Auto + Homeowners/Renters Insurance. If you rent, It is usually only cost $100 to $200 a year and can cover up to $35,000 of personal items.

- Monthly Insurance Cost :

Net Income : This is how much is left for you to live on after you have paid for all the above-mentioned expense categories. How much is payed to all these non-tangible expenses may be very frustrating. These may not validate the most recent popular trends or be the next trending tweet, but will enable you to pay taxes regularly, protect yourself, and personal items from accidents while saving for your future. Fundamentally these habits make up the core of any stable budget and lifestyle. Others may disagree but without more involved personal discussion about your financial situation this is all I would recommend and is a safe place to start.

<u>Housing Expenses</u> : How much you pay monthly in rent or to your mortgage lender. The general rule of thumb is you should not spend more than 15% of your gross income on your rent/mortgage + utilities.

- Monthly Rent / Mortgage Cost :

<u>Loan Payments</u> : Monthly payments to various personal debts. The goal is to have no personal debts, but today's expectations impose that you need the newest and greatest of whatever your credit score can get you. This approach will likely never make you a dime! One way to work with the credit card lenders is to use credit cards that give you benefits to stores that you already frequent. The key is to always pay them off each month, and never carry a balance. Then you reap the rewards without paying interest. Drive used cars, buy clothing you can afford, wait to take a trip until you have the cash. It may take years to get there but you will be in a secure financial position then that you will thank yourself then!! Paying minimum payments will not get you ahead and you will pay far more in your total payments vs how much you owe today. Taking a minor lifestyle

compromise today will put you in a far better position in your financial future.

- Total Personal Loan Balance :

- Total Monthly Loan Payments :

Avg Interest Rate = Sum of All Loan(s) Interest Rates / # of Loans

- Average Loan Interest Rate :

Food Expenses : How much you spend on your typical meals and snacks each week. Location and convenience preference will drive how much this will cost you. Grocery shopping and making the majority of your work week meals at home will help you minimize your reoccurring expenses. Next step would be to refine your grocery list to the items you like, that are not expensive. If you live near a bulk grocery store that could be a good option to minimize expenses if buying in bulk works for you. Real social status is not determined by where you buy your groceries. Food co-ops are a good alternative to support local farms and typically are cost leaders to typical grocery stores. But co-ops may deliver a wide variety produce seasonally than you can use on a given week, so adapt your meal plan to use what is available and not waste food.

- Weekly Food Expenses :

Savings : How much you deposit into your savings account from your checking account each month. Savings accounts have a slightly higher annual percentage yield (APY) interest rate so your money can grow faster in comparison to your checking account. Neither should be considered a growth account compared to actual investment funds. Work towards depositing four to six months of expenses into your checking account. This is a safe bank balance to maintain to prepare you for any future emergencies or unexpected expenses.

- How Much You Save Monthly :

Retirement / Investments : How much you contribute to your retirement investment fund monthly before and after tax. If you start 35 or 40 years before you plan to retire you could experience a return or growth factor of 5 to 7 times what you invest over that time. With typical market performance over that period of time. The earlier your start the more stable your retirement fund will be. Regularly contributing 15% or more of your income is recommended. Potential exceptions to this recommendation would be while you are a full-time college student, any money you do make while in college needs to be focused on supporting your education. This will help you pass classes and pay for college reducing how much you may take out in student loans, increasing how much of your future income will be available for enabling your desired lifestyle.

- Employer Match % :

- Your Yearly Investment % :

<u>Utilities</u> : How much you pay to keep the gas, water, electricity, trash, recycling, internet, phone, cable TV every month. This category can be expensive, but you typically cannot go live in a cabin in the woods to save money and still function today. Find the right balance of reasonable compromises to your current expectations and don't let short term gains distract you from what is best for your

future! Save where you can, it all adds up.

- Monthly Utilities
    - Electric :
    - Gas :
    - Cable :
    - Water :
    - Trash :
    - Phone :
    - Total Monthly Utilities :

Fuel Expenses : How much you spend to fuel your car to get back and forth to your job(s) and around town. Estimate how many miles you drive your car each year and your typical fuel millage.

- Estimated Miles Per Year :

- Estimated MPG :

- Price of Gas :

Lifestyle Expenses : What do you do each month that is not routine, going out to dinner, movies, bowling, date night, road trips, online purchases, basically stuff you don't buy on a regular basis. Estimate how much you spend and see if your budget is balanced.

- Weekly Fun Money :

3.5 Your Budget Summary

The order of this summary page matches the linked spreadsheet for your convenience.

- Gross Income :
- Effective Federal Tax Rate :
- Effective State Tax Rate :
- Medicare Tax Rate :
- Social Security Tax Rate :
- Monthly
    - Health Care Cost :
    - Auto & Home Insurance Cost :
    - Rent / Mortgage Cost :
- Personal Loans
    - Total Balance :
    - Monthly Payment :
    - Average Interest Rate :
- Weekly Food Expenses :
- Monthly Personal Savings :
- Investments

  - Personal Investment % :
  - Employer Match % :
- Utilities
  - Electric :
  - Gas :
  - Cable + Streaming :
  - Water :
  - Trash :
  - Phone :
- Fuel
  - Average MPG :
  - Miles Driven Each Year :
  - Price of Gas :
- Weekly Fun Money :

3.6 Success Pointers

1. Spend time with those who supportyou, if they don't; then don't waste your time
    - You will learn this lesson several times over time
2. Have a consistent sleep schedule
3. Exercise regularly for your health and confidence
4. Work as much as you can consistently supportwithout becoming run down
5. Do not take out personal loans if at all possible
6. Invest 15 % of your income in mutual funds for retirement. Start early, never withdrawal until you have fully retired!
7. Don't envy someone else's perceived success, they fight battles they don't share
8. Only buy if you have saved for it

9. Eliminate unneeded expenses and monthly subscriptions
10. Purchase only what prepares you for your future
11. Pay credit cards off at the end of every month
12. Only purchase used cars with cash to avoid the initial depreciation and auto loan interest burden
13. Save up at least a six-month emergency fund in your savings account, equal to size times how much you spend every month
14. Avoid paying interest in all cases, excluding a home mortgage. Rent to minimize financial risk until you can comfortably place a 20 % down-payment on a home you want. Be very picky it is all about Location, Location, Location!

3.7 Budget to Better You

Implementing your new budget and adjusting habits may take time to become second nature. Be patient and reflect on why you are making this change, it is to help YOUR future. This is not selfish. It is smart and responsible to plan ahead, and not just wing it. I once heard a quote from an unknown source saying "we work all week to work against our self on the weekend"... After processing this statement, I had several realizations about how I was not helping myself develop when I had the most control over my time and commitments. You may have several observations as well about your current or past habits and if they help or prevent you from achieving a better tomorrow. Don't rush this process. All good things take time and effort to achieve.

Expecting immediate perfection may make this financial approach exhausting and potentially work against you by compromising your mental health. Let your constructive financial habits build over time with small corrections vs drastic changes so you are comfortable with your new lifestyle. Realize you are in control of your future and all the opportunities and responsibilities within it! Success is the byproduct of a good plan and consistent progress. Now that you have a good budget which follows the proposed guidelines, it is up to you to be consistent about following it. Record your current thoughts below for future reference. Will be interesting how grateful your future self may feel by your decisions today.

The Author

Growing up in suburbia west Michigan and being voted most likely to succeed unexpectedly by my high school graduation class. I should have started to realize I had a different work ethic than most. Shortly thereafter I joined an emerging leaders' program at Western Michigan University broadening my social awareness and leadership toolbox and applied my leadership skills while pursing my B.S. in Aerospace Engineering in various capacities as a student. I spent the majority of my free time with our competitive radio-controlled aircraft design build fly team, as a student leadership retreat facilitator and occasional seminar speaker at student events. Learning invaluable teamwork and social problem-solving experience. Once complete I worked full time for a few years then returned to pursue my M.S. in Aerospace Engineering, primarily to refine my ability to contribute to future projects more effectively. Each step was an investment toward my future, paying it forward as often as I could. I chose my Aerospace Engineering path at the age of 13 and never questioned my choice... It felt natural and energizing with every step or leap forward. It was not until after I received my master's degree, did I truly realize how impactful my decision and dedication was at such a young age. Part of that realization was why I wrote this book, to help others realize how important each day of their life really is. It is easy to forget how valuable our time is, and how quickly we give it away. I hope you finish this book and find yourself eager for tomorrow, overflowing with a sense of humble self-worth empowering you to chase your dreams.

Why Write A Book

I want to help you succeed and be content with your life. Pursue what adds value to your life, while adding value to others lives along the way. Unfortunately, it is not practical to meet all of you and share what I know so far, but I can at least document what I know today and share it with you so you can benefit too. We all interpret our insecurities differently because we are all unique and have different proverbial tools available to defuse them. I see so many have their insecurities unknowingly used against them and I want you to be aware and actively curate your life. Your life is worth investing in, average habits won't do. Be the outlier and passionate while pursuing a life that you value. The view from the top will be better knowing you built it.

Don't let the talk end here, go walk your walk.

Honest Feedback

Tell me what you think about any part of the book by leaving a review on Amazon. Tag questions / comments @SegardPublishing on Instagram or via email feedback@segardpublishing.com. I welcome your input with an open mind.

Made in the USA
Columbia, SC
22 December 2021